No Barking in the Hallways

To Billy,
Here's to
more compassion
in teaching!

No Barking
in the Hallways

Poems from the Classroom

Ann Bracken

Ann Bracken

 NEW ACADEMIA
PUBLISHING

Washington, DC

Library of Congress Control Number: 2016954977
ISBN 978-0-9981477-0-3 paperback (alk. paper)

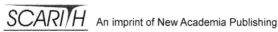 An imprint of New Academia Publishing

 New Academia Publishing
4401-A Connecticut Avenue NW #236, Washington DC 20008
info@newacademia.com - www.newacademia.com

For my children—my greatest teachers—Brian and Christella

"How can the extinguished light be lit again,
so that teachers and learners can appear before one another and show,
in speech and action, who they are and what they can do?"

~Maxine Greene, *Releasing the Imagination*

Contents

Acknowledgments

"Liam Sits Folded," *Praxilla*, 2011

"Naptime in the Kindergarten Room," *Pif*, 2014

"Value-Added Teachers," *New Verse News*, 2014

"Rena," *Mipoesias*, 2015

"Everything's Fine," Freshman's Lament," and "Save Yourself a
    Phone Call," *Dragonfly*, 2016

"The Autoworker Explains How the Factory Works," *ArLiJo*, 2016

I would like to thank the following people for believing in my work
and their unflagging support: Grace Cavalieri, Patricia VanAmburg,
Jane Nitsch, Gerry Cohee, Renee Rogers, and all the members of my
meditation group. I would also like to thank Kate Schruefer for her
story that inspired the title poem "No Barking in the Hallways."

Preface

Since I began teaching back in 1974, two guiding principles have informed my work: finding a way to connect with the students and using creative and engaging presentations to help them learn. When I was a speech pathology undergraduate, my professors at Towson University presented me with a fundamental piece of advice about teaching methods: "Do whatever works to help the children succeed."

That single dictum provided a loose framework for all of the lessons I planned. In the initial years of my career when I was teaching elementary-school children, doing whatever worked meant winning my students with games, puzzles, and dramatic play. As a result, most of them loved working with the "speech lady" as they used to call me. They had fun. And they learned. So years later when I began to teach writing and English classes, I looked forward to planning activities that would make the learning process fun.

But in the early 2000s when I had returned to a formal classroom setting, there were new recommendations for teachers to follow: raise the scores, use the data to plan your lessons. Instead of teaching as if I were assembling a colorful collage, I had to teach as if I were filling in columns of numbers on a spreadsheet.

I noticed that the more the education system focused on data collection and test scores, the less creative teachers felt they could be. Teachers framed lessons around discrete skills that they knew were on the standardized exams. Administrators tied evaluations to test scores, erasing the teacher's incentive to extend and expand on concepts that resonated with students. Fewer art projects, more drills.

I began to see the loss of joy in my students' faces and the loss of joy in my colleagues' classrooms. More testing led to more stress. And oftentimes, the children who couldn't pass the tests were the special education students with whom I worked. But all students and teachers are being crushed by rigid expectations and standardized tests. Their stories inspire my poetry.

Value-Added Teachers

We feel frustrated
as we rumble around in cramped offices
with all the people shouting
Words don't matter.
Especially when we hear graduates
of the university
referred to as output.

When people become output
there's no need for nurture.
Sewage pipes have output,
as do factories that churn out row after row
of standardized parts.

In cramped classrooms and windowless lecture halls,
teachers are gauged by their productivity—
here every human complexity is reduced
to a series of data points, quantified and measured
success or failure—positive or negative output.

These days we no longer relish
seeing joy or surprise or the flash
of an ah-ha moment on our students' faces.
Instead of planning a field trip to the meadow
for a sensory experience,
we spend time trying to quantify
commitment, measure amazement,
determine a cut score for
how much inspiration is needed
for a journey into the unknown.

Abe the Man Boy

Abe the man boy cruises into the classroom,
reciting his litany of lateness.

I'm too tired for this writin' jazz;
had to take my sister to daycare.

Abe from Sierra Leone knows war's haunting face
as well as he knows the latest Def Jam rhymes
or Ravens' football plays.

War's messed up.
It don't solve nothin'.

But when Abe reads an essay, his swagger dissolves.
I never had any reading help. My mom got me outta the country
when I was eight or nine.

The soldiers almost kidnapped me.
Abe is a junior in high school — reads at the third-grade level.

I do all right on that multiple choice stuff,
but I'm lost when I gotta read a whole book.

When I take his case to the supervisor, she tells me,
"Abe doesn't have time to take reading. If he wants to graduate,
he needs two foreign language credits — in one year.
We've got him in Spanish and Italian."

All They Want Is Another Option

The boys fold white sheets of looseleaf
into paper airplanes with sleek wings.
The only passengers are the complaints
about their expiring chances to pass the graduation tests.

They sit at their desks as if drowning in bucket seats
of meaningless terms like mood and tone.
But when we flee the classroom and
commandeer the parking lot for flight testing

their planes soar high and far, like powder in the wind.
The boys shout out their dreams
as if to boost the acceleration of their jets.
If only the timbre of their hopes

could outwit the arbitrary
prison of the classroom.
Who can't see their mechanical genius
in the circling planes?

Angie at Five

Her brown curls never touch a brush,
her gait clumsy as she skips down the hall
wearing scuffed Mary Janes with one green sock and one blue.
She smiles and hands me a pink rose wrapped in a wet paper towel.

Too young to be wary of teachers, Angie tells me,
My momma says we ain't got no money to buy me shoes right now.
Anyways, I jus' go barefoot all summer long. But sometimes when I play
in the field 'hind our 'partment, I git all cut up from them
glass bottles those big kids leave lyin' 'round.
Her accent a rhythmic fusion of Richmond's streets and Appalachian hills

When I think of Angie now—years after her kindergarten speech class,
I don't wonder if she ever learned to say *sssnake, sssilly, or ssscoot…*
I wonder if she has a job and if…
she is growing roses.

Andy's Breakthrough

Over in the corner of the special ed kindergarten room
sits a suction machine I use four times a day
to clear Monica's tracheotomy.
Tucked away in the closet—diapers
in case Robbie has an accident.
I have eight students and an assistant
until the morning Andy arrives with a note pinned to his overalls.

> *Hi! I'm Andy and I don't talk.*
> *Here's what you can say so I understand*
> *colors and numbers.*
> *Red =mommy's coat*
> *Blue =daddy's truck*
> *One = cat*
> *Two = balloons*

The list goes on for all the colors and the numbers up to 10.
That note rocks me hard
like a shove from behind
when you're first learning to ice skate.

One January day after snow and ice cancel recess
for the third day in a row
my class of pop-go-the weasel five-year-olds destroys my calm—
Everybody sit down, I yell.

Andy jumps up in the back of the room and smiles
like he's found a new puppy,
then points his finger at me and announces, "Bracken angrrrrrry."

The class erupts with laughter.
Andy jumps up and repeats "Bracken angrrrry" over and over.
The kids dance and jump around the room
chanting Andy's words like the chorus of a new song.
I join in.

Billy Follows Me Outside the Psych Hospital Classroom

Some days at lunchtime
I walk the perimeter
of the school parking lot,
arms swinging, legs pumping,
racing to restore inner
balance before afternoon classes.

Some days I sit outside the school on a stone bench
framed by yellow forsythia bushes,
aching for solitude.
I escape the dark hallways,
the girl pounding on the door,
the boy weeping in the "quiet" room.

Some days Billy with the curly, red hair
and the keen gaze follows me outside.
"You're not going to stay much longer," he tells me.
I eat my sandwich.
Why do you say that?
"I can just tell."

Sometimes I still see Billy's face, that mysterious boy
who raised his brother and helped me teach sewing.
How did he know?
I wonder, should I have confessed?
"I just know you're leaving. My dad left us and I can tell.
Mrs. Green left last year. She was just like you."
I curse my transparent eyes and ask,
What do you mean?

"You're too gentle for a place like this.
I guess we'll have a party for you when you leave."

Drumming in English Class

Meg and I taught a ninth-grade English class together —
she demanded order and precision. I craved spontaneity.

One boy — Magic — was especially interesting to watch.
I knew his diagnosis — attention deficit hyperactivity disorder — ADHD.

Magic lived with his aunt and uncle;
both of his parents had serious drinking problems

and could no longer care for him. My conclusion?
Magic's ADHD was perfectly understandable.

Magic was bright, creative, and he wanted to do well in school.
But he forgot things — like notebook paper and handing in assignments.

On days when the class was playful, engaged, and excited,
Meg demanded that I rein in the kids.

Whenever Meg crammed the lid down on the class,
the drumming would start — Magic was the radar.

Meg threatened the class — "There may be two quizzes tomorrow"
and "I see much more homework for the weekend."

Students put their heads down,
rolled pencils back and forth on their desks, fiddled with backpacks, cell phon

The cacophony of random movement in the classroom
leads to rote behavior management of "hyperactive" kids.

We punish them, reprimand them,
change their seats, up their medications.

Endless High School, Recurring Nightmare

Bill finished Algebra I at the end of tenth grade,
passed with a low D.
He took the algebra test in May and failed it,
just like he has failed the other three graduation tests.

In September,
Bill takes an algebra mastery class —
a fancy name for a class where he repeats practice tests
to re-learn what he missed.

Wait a minute...
if Bill has failed all four tests, he can't possibly graduate in four years,
even with summer school...
"Not a problem," says the guidance counselor —
"Bill's on the six-year plan."

That's a good one, the six-year plan.
But Bill's already nineteen.
I shake my head and sip my coffee.
Really, what are we doing for Bill?

"He can take two mastery classes
per semester and then retake the tests twice
or three times this year."

I want to say, *But he keeps failing!*
The same tests!
Over and over.

The guidance counselor reads my mind and assures me,
"If he doesn't pass, he can always do
a bridge project."

I ask the obvious questions:
Why doesn't Bill get an exemption?
Why is a cognitively impaired student taking the
same graduation tests as everyone else?

In Maryland cognitively impaired students
earn only a certificate of attendance, not a diploma.
If Bill doesn't pass the tests,
he won't earn a diploma.

"Bill's mother won't agree
to label him," the counselor explains.
"She wants him to get a diploma."

Somehow, Bill passed the required courses
with lots of help, even extra credit.
No Fs on Bill's transcript—
an ugly game administrators force
teachers to play.

I look at his scores on the tests, all well below the passing mark.
The lower the scores, the more projects required.
And the projects require one-on-one assistance.
How many bridge projects does Bill need?

"Bill must do
eleven bridge projects
to graduate. He's got two years left."

Francie's Scarlet Letter

Francie the bad-ass girl
slumps into English class every day,
pants hugging her muffin-topped hips,
red hair spiked and short, fingernails neon green.
From her seat in the back of the room, Francie asks,
You know that story of the Scarlet Letter?
I wear one too—
My A is for adopted.

Her binder is covered with graffiti phrases
"I hate to read." "I can't write." The word "Loser"
scrawled
up the spine and onto the front cover.
One day Francie blurts out in the middle of writing an essay,
My real mom had drug problems.
That's why she gave me away.

On her way out the door,
Francie passes me her crumpled homework assignment:

Haiku
I just want to be
good enough for my new mom
to love me.

Francie sucks on her fingers
as she walks on down the hall.

Freshman's Lament

Because no one saw him steal in the side entrance
and creep into the locker room

that echoed with the silence of steel boxes.
Because no one saw him grab the girl

as she stuffed her blue gym suit into a duffle bag.
Because no one saw him shove her to the floor

and steal her freshman smile.
Because no one heard her cry echo through the deserted basement.

Because all the mysteries of sex and power were twined for us,
as inseparable as the white laces of our saddle shoes,

we blamed *her* for what happened. All that year, we whispered and jeered
smug in our little homeroom cliques.

Who would want to have sex with her?
She's so plain. And she's fat.

I wish I could hold her now, apologize
for all I didn't understand

about violence and force and shame.
I'd sit with her at lunch time, promise to stand by her.

Give her back
her innocence.

Green Tea and Gingersnaps

Frayed sweatshirts litter the worn carpet of the classroom floor.
Boys read *Of Mice and Men,* stopping after every few paragraphs,
mocking the characters Candy and Crooks,
whistling low when Curly's wife flirts with Slim.

I sip on raspberry green tea. Take deep breaths.
Sigh to calm myself.
Too early in the spring to open dust-covered windows.
Out of anemic excuses,
I surrender to their daily chant of
"We want green tea. Give us green tea."

I give in, not knowing where I'm headed.
Circle your desks, I say, *we're having a tea party.*
One condition hangs in the air
like a waning moon in the dawn sky,
You still have to read.

These same boys who cuss at each other,
who scrawl obscenities on the board when I turn my back
now pass cookies and pour tea
as if they're guests in my home.

They relax into the story as they read.
When I serve them green tea and gingersnaps,
it's as if we see each other for the first time.

Helen with Piercings

Helen speaks just above a whisper, smiles shyly when saying hello.
Her spikey black hair fringes out from under a purple fedora,
a wide leopard-print belt hugs her marshmallow middle.

Helen with piercings works slowly and deliberately
on every reading task, never asks questions—
even when she doesn't understand.

She blends in with other freshmen
wearing leggings and green or purple nail polish.
She struggles with pronouncing basic words—ambition, interaction—

and explaining plot details. She doodles on her paper
when I ask her to write. *I'm not good at writing.*
And I don't read much, but I want to. Before she writes

about the characters in *The House on Mango Street,*
Helen opens her art portfolio and shares sketches
of the book's characters. *I love Manga,*

so my characters have that same quality.
Here's my sketch of Sofia.
She has flowers on her shirt to symbolize her innocence.

Jorge carries a magnifying glass
in his back pocket.
He questions every detail.

Horace at Fifteen

Horace made the JV football team, but
he forgets the plays, argues with the coach,
falls asleep during practice.
Horace lumbers into my reading class
every day at 8:10, slides into his seat,
props his head on his Ravens backpack. About half-way through class
Horace asks to go to the health room—stomach pains again.
The health room nurse tells me he's been there
twenty-four times this semester.

Size? Above average. Reading level? First grade.
Horace wears team jerseys every day, keeps his new
Air Jordans white, red laces untied. Almost starts a fight when
someone scuffs his shoes. Horace beats out the rhythms to every new
hip hop song, likes the girls. He dreams of having his own business.
*First I'll work for my uncle, like I done this summer. I can lay carpet
all day. My uncle even paid me $50 a week.*

In the library, Horace grabs a book with Michael Jordan on the cover,
then sprawls on a beanbag chair. After a few minutes, he tosses the book
over to me. *I'm too tired to read. Besides, I already know
about Michael Jordan. Any comic books in here?*

Invisible Walls

DeMonte shuffles into the classroom
a sliver before tardy

mumbling as he slides into his chair
"Stop starin' at me, lady, I ain't done nothin'."

We look at each other and wait.
"My disability might make me punch you out."

His institutional phrasing—the reference to his disability—
signals me that he knows the system's code words.

DeMonte drums his pencil and searches the room,
poised as if waiting for someone hiding in the shadows.

When the characters in the play we're reading
 talk about society's food chain of rich and poor,

DeMonte shakes his head in disagreement.
"We don' eat in no fast food places," he tells me.

When another character says he's gone from
being a Santa to being a Scrooge,

I ask if DeMonte knows the story.
"No," his umber eyes flash daggers in my direction.

"But if anybody call me that, I'm gonna beat his face in.
That just sounds nasty."

How do I reach this boy? I don't want to be
another teacher who fails him. Who offers dry bones instead of a feast.

DeMonte slams his book closed—
"I ain't readin' no more."

It's Not Like That

Emma's in and out of my classroom and
always sits up front. Straight blond hair,
a pincer-like grip on the pen as she takes notes.
Blue blotches under her makeup.

Emma comes in for a meeting and checks her phone—
I can't help but notice cracks in the glass.
See bruises covering her arms and legs.
How did you get those? I ask.

"I drank too much—slipped and fell on the wet porch. I'm such a klutz."
I know this story—the rage,
then the apology, the promises, the make-up sex.
I know the way it repeats in ever-tightening cycles.

Before Emma can speak, I say, *It's confusing being with someone
who hurts you and then apologizes.*
I hand her a brochure with a help-line number
and a checklist of warning signs.

She bursts into tears. "My parents think the same thing.
But it's not like that."
I nod.
Emma chokes back a sob.
"I'm OK. But thank you." She tucks the booklet
deep into her backpack.

Emma misses our scheduled conference. Never explains.
Now she sits near the door,
leaves every day
before class ends.

Jake and His Mother

Jake sits at a table instead of a desk
and shouts
sexual things that would make a grown man gag—
to say Jake is inappropriate is just edu-babble
masking my discomfort.
But some things make me want to laugh
if only I weren't standing up in front of a bunch of adolescent boys
who study my posture and my face.
We don't know what to do with Jake
as we plan for graduation.
Will he tell a crude joke on stage?
Will he talk about his ass? Or the girl he "did" over the weekend?
One day I meet Jake and his mother
on their way to a family therapy session.
I introduce myself and extend my hand.
Jake's mother frowns and pulls hers away
saying, "Watch the hand."

Juking the Stats

The Incident

Milton shuffles into the classroom, lays his head on the desk,
burying his face in an Orioles sweatshirt.
He mumbles, *I'm sick. Leave me alone.*

"Milton, what's the matter?" He moans, *I'm sick. Just leave me alone.*
Erring on the side of caution, I hand him a pass
for the health room, encourage him to go.

Milton shoots out of his chair, yanks his backpack off the floor,
backhands me in the chest.
Get outta my way, lady.

The Meeting

Judith, the assistant principal, paces back and forth behind her desk.
"Would you like some chocolate? How about fruit?
I always eat when I get upset."

I'm way beyond chocolate, Judith.
No student has ever assaulted me.
I sit down, my hands trembling.

"Well, we've heard of this happening with Milton at home.
I guess you want to fill out an incident report? Judith pulls up the form
on her computer. "But please, don't call it an assault."

Milton backhanded me in the chest.
He hit me. What else
do you want me to call it?

20

Judith clicks on a dropdown menu of infractions.
I read the choices:
Discourtesy, contempt, rudeness, disregard,
disrespect, insolence, impudence.

"Pick any one of these. Just don't call it an assault.
We have to file this report with the central office.
They're watching our stats."

Julio Eats Breakfast in Reading Class

Julio wears new jeans and an Eminem tee shirt.
He pounds out hip hop rhythms on his desk.
I plead, "Please, can we just get through this story?"
Julio chugs a twenty-ounce Monster energy drink,
then jumps in front of me and balls his fists.
What do you mean by that? You tryin' to say I'm a loser?
Before I can protest, he shouts a line from a song,
Don't push me 'cause I'm close to the edge,
then lays more beats on the desk-turned-drum.
Your stories are lame. Wanna hear mine? Of course you don't
but I'm gonna tell you anyway. Julio perches on the edge of his chair,
leans back, opens and closes his fists in quick succession.
I went out with my dad last night. You ever heard of this game?
His friends poured beer into a funnel. My dad chugged it through a tube.
Then he fell off the chair. Julio's laugh is hollow.
We don't know where he is now. My words stick in my throat,
he doesn't register the sorrow on my face.
Julio pulls out a bag of Doritos.
Can I eat now? My mom didn't make me any breakfast.

Lenny Dreams of His Future

Lenny nods his head in time to the rap-infused vocabulary lesson.
I'm tired, he tells me. *My pencil's all the way*
in the bottom of my backpack. He digs in the bulging red sack,
papers confetti the floor. *You wanna hear 'bout my life?*
Oh, yeah, oh yeah, I know you do, I see you smilin'.
Lenny shakes his head back and forth, moving in time to the beat
of his inner metronome. *I been to seven different schools in seven years.*
Every time we move I gotta start this reading crap again. Even in high school.
Lenny rubs lotion on his arms. *I visited my dad up in Massachusetts*
on Saturday. He's thirty— doin' time for drugs. Saw my sister Ashley—
she's seventeen. Having twins. Lenny tosses the lotion up in the air, catches
it backhanded, and slams it into his backpack. *Score! My goal?*
I wanna be a dad by the time I'm eighteen.

Liam Sits Folded

Liam sits folded on the floor
outside my classroom,
his six-foot frame crumpled
like a discarded origami bird.
Liam waits next to the lockers,
with his backpack propping him up—
head back, mouth open, eyes closed.
Every day he wears too-short pants,
shirts faded and full of holes,
and white, threadbare socks.

Liam's glasses, thick and brown,
help him make sense of what he reads,
but can't provide the necessary clues
to help decipher a grin from a grimace.
Without words of explanation,
Liam sees threats instead of invitations.

I can't do this, he tells me,
stabbing the end of a yellow, lead pencil
over and over again into his arm.
When I reach my hand out to stop him,
Liam smiles in relief.
I really don't want to hurt myself, he tells me.
I just get so frustrated,
and the stabbing starts again.

Liam sits folded at his desk,
feet tucked up under him,
backpack ever strapped and sagging on his back.
Folded into his world of contradictions are

piles of papers
with words running together
like melting crayons.
Yet when he draws a cartoon figure,
I instantly recognize it as
Mama from *A Raisin in the Sun*.
See this? The plant in the picture stands for hope,
Liam tells me.
To everyone else, it's a worthless, scraggly stalk with leaves.
But to Mama—it's a rich, red geranium.

Lisa's Truth

Lisa, my supervisor, charges into my classroom
at the end of the day,
the jangling of her silver Chico's necklace
announces her arrival.

"I've been looking at the grades online—
why is your ninth-grade class doing so poorly?"
*They never finish their classwork and then they don't do any of the
homework I assign…*
"So stop giving homework." Lisa
adjusts her jacket to cover her breasts.
"What else?"

Well, it seems futile to teach them Romeo and Juliet.…
Cheryl speaks broken English, and she reads at the first-grade level.
Sharon and Steve are cognitively impaired…
Tim walks around the room and sharpens his pencil every ten minutes.…
Lisa twists her necklace into a tight knot,
"Let them watch the movie."
But how is that meeting their needs?
How does that improve their reading?

Lisa pulls her jacket closed and picks up her clipboard.
"Well, teaching reading is fine,
you can do that during lunch if you want.
But they're in an English class,
so just cover the curriculum. Show the movie."
She heads for the door and then looks back at me,
"And make up a test they can pass."

We dive into the story—watching the movie scene by scene,
role-playing, making maps of the town,
drawing pictures of characters, even making masks.
They have a study guide and a test that nearly matches it.
Some of the kids inch by with grades in the 60s,
but Lisa gloats when she sees me.
"See, they all passed. Aren't you happy?"

Lydia's Choice

There wasn't much difference between us—
Lydia older by a year
Louisiana born
me from Maryland—
two branches struggling
on the same tree of duty.
We taught the students
who drew the short straws of chance
who couldn't pass the English graduation test
filled with tenses and tone,
heavy pages of elusive sonnets.
Our class was their last chance.

Lydia and I shared our life's secrets—
the curse of our difficult marriages,
my choice to leave, hers to stay.
Often after work,
I found Lydia alone at her desk
grading towers of essays,
her car the last one to leave the lot.

One day Lydia confided
she'd had enough of his cheating,
his lies about money, and his
flimsy faith. *He never really found the Lord,*
was all she said.
I'm leaving that man.
Now Lydia smiled more,
almost danced, left work early.
We planned a celebration.

But somehow the blisters on her heart
fused into a familiar
pattern of pain,
a tattered lace of failed promises.
Once again, Lydia's car the last one on the lot.
She never has time to talk anymore—
shuts her door at the end of the day.

Lyle's Dignity

The first day of reading class Lyle's hand grips the pencil,
tongue traces back and forth over his lips.
He prints in large, wobbly block letters,
"My name is Lyle. I am fifteen. I like high school."
Lyle peeks at me through corn-silk straight bangs and smiles.
His teeth misaligned like the crooked pickets of an abandoned fence.
The theme of the books we read,
Lyle tells me, *is the need for positive role models.*
Like the puzzles he draws on his notebooks,
Lyle's life is full of missing pieces and jagged edges:
high-school-dropout mom who cusses at him,
eight-year-old brother who trashes classrooms and bruises shins.
Like the last cookie on a plate, I offer my meager smile. One day
Lyle declares, *I know I'm intelligent. Even my doctor tells me that.*
Ain't nobody can take away my dignity.

Maggie Gets a PRN
(PRN: a medical term meaning pro re nata, or drugs as needed)

In the psych hospital high school where I teach, I glimpse Maggie out of
the corner of my eye as she floats into my food and nutrition class looking
for chocolate chip cookies. Her buddy Shana with her—locking arms as
they enter the room.
Maggie's eyes tell me her body is there
but her spirit still cruises in a car with Primal Fear's latest song blasting.
Then I see the safety pin stuck through her left eyebrow.
"I'm punk now," Maggie screams and all the other kids laugh. I notice a
faint, red line on her neck, as if she had wiped off some blood.

The only behavior management techniques they teach us
in the psych hospital are the standard carrots and sticks—
awarding high fives for good behavior and calling security for bad.
An eyebrow-piercing demands another response. I play it cool.

When did you get this piercing? I haven't seen it before.
"Shana and I snuck out of math class when Billy turned off all the lights.
I wanted to pierce my eyebrow, but my mom said no. Too late now."

Maggie wanders around the room, walking away from me. I weave
through the maze of desks, trying to get close enough to reason with her.
What about infection? Doesn't it hurt?
How did you pierce yourself with such a big safety pin?

"I'm fine," Maggie insists, eyes glazing over
as she wiggles the pin in her reddened eyebrow.
"Ewww…it feels a little hot." She giggles and pokes Shana.
"I think I'll go see the nurse for some Valium—PRN."
Maggie and Shana move more quickly,
now that they're off to see the nurse. I had never heard the term before,
but suddenly it all made sense. PRN. As needed.
And Maggie needs some pain relief.

31

After class ends, I clean up the room and get ready for the next day. I can't stop thinking about Maggie. No one waits for her when she gets home; no one cooks her dinner or takes her shopping for clothes. Maggie's not a bad kid. She's a kid in pain. I was hoping she'd get some Tylenol and an ice pack.

But here in the psych hospital, the pain relief is all legal and comes delivered in little white cups from the hands of the nurse. It's the only place I know that would give a kid with a throbbing, red, newly-pierced eyebrow a hit of Valium. PRN.

Marcus Speaks

The day he showed up
I found a note on my desk:
"New student today.
He's non-verbal."

I treated Marcus
like everyone else.
Invited his introduction.

He glared,
towered over the others,
shoved his papers onto the floor and
barked.

The other boys laughed.
Marcus barked again
ending with a low growl.
Even in a psych hospital

a boy who barks is threatening.
Every day, Marcus scowled
paced in the back of the room
sometimes whimpering
low and soft, like a wounded puppy,

sometimes leaping in front of
a laughing classmate.
Wailing or yelping—
scaring him into silence.

The psychiatrist had no answers—
the behavior specialist shrugged.
One day, Marcus dropped his homework on my desk
and barked in my face.

That sounds like
an angry bark to me.
I locked eyes with Marcus—
he grinned.

Then he said,
"Can you move my seat?

Martin Who Swaggers

Martin rides his rage like a tormented tiger,
hiding his fears beneath stripes of cold and mean.
I don't trust you, he roars
then slams his rock fist on my wobbling desk.
Everything is too hard.
Everything you want is too much.
He tosses his last excuse like a gnarled bone—
I can't work with you today, lady. I got a hangover.
Martin paces and prowls as if those moves
hold the key to his freedom. He springs at me
if I inch too close. Martin charms when he wants something,
cuts deals if I'll listen, then tears up the contract
and throws the pieces in my face.

Marvene Teaches Reading

Most days, she teaches, while I grit my teeth
and cajole the students into behaving.
Like sudden storms that rise out of a desert,
Marvene's dark moods descend without much warning.
She never shares daily plans.
One day she announces, "All of you read at about the third-grade level,
so I brought a third-grade book today."
The high school students—all taller than either of us—
squirm, put their heads down, and murmur dirty jokes to each other.
My stomach knots when Marvene closes her book,
stands over Kenny as he fidgets.
She predicts, "You'll never amount to anything."
He leans back in his chair. *So what?*
My mother's taking me outta this dumb reading class.
Marvene glares at him and shouts, "You might as well slit your throat."
Maybe I will, Kenny says. He wipes his eyes as he storms out of the room.

Marvene returns nine days later. No explanation. She frowns
when I tell her the lessons I've covered while she was gone.
I sense the storm now and try to flee with the last student.
I grab the doorknob, turn it quickly, take one step into the hallway
when Marvene's voice fires across the room.
"I just want to know what good you think you can do
teaching those low kids Latin roots? Is that even in the curriculum?"
I nod and keep walking. Her eyes turn to stone,
her lips rigid. She fires another barrage.
"Where did you get those lessons? Those kids don't need that stuff."
Marvene moves closer. My heart pounds and my mind repeats
over and over, *Tell her to stop. Tell her she can't talk to you like that.*
She inches closer to me. I freeze.
My brain and my mouth out of sync.

My heart thunders in my chest, like a rabbit fleeing a hound. All I can say, *I have to go to my next class.*

Maxine the Hugger

When Maxine enters the speech room
she always throws her arms around my neck.
Today she pulls my face close to her cheek. Her party dress
is dotted with food stains, the gray-white collar frayed
and limp. Maxine smells like musty sheets
draped over furniture in an abandoned house.
Blond bangs graze the tops of her brows, thick lashes
frame hopeful eyes. As if to answer the question
I would never ask, Maxine tells me, *We don't have no water
in our house.* She reads the worry on my face.
*But Momma says not to fret
'cause my Uncle Todd—he lives two houses down—
he's gonna run a hose to our place.*

Mythology

When I write on the board
in front of my students,
sometimes I freeze inside
still haunted by the Gorgon-like teacher in my past.

I remember Medusa, her head full of snakes,
her gaze that turned you to stone.
Then I remember my own Medusa.
I remember Sister Bertha.

Her clipped tones and mocking stare
turned my hands to ice—
my stomach to a vortex of fear.
My brain so unmoored from the words on the page

that I made up the stories instead of translating them.
Sr. Bertha, more Gorgon than the myth.
As we stood at the board, translating from Latin to English
she unleashed her daily harangue.

You have no right to talk to me like that—
you don't know how much I study,
drilling those word-lists night after night.

My classmates look shocked.
What makes you think we're all lazy? One mistake and you yell.
Maybe you should be kinder.

Maybe it was the way Sr. Bertha praised Perseus' bravery
or his clever use of Athena's shield,
to sneak past the hissing Gorgon—

Something in that myth urged me to turn from
another moment of blackboard shame
and slay the Gorgon sister with my words.

Naptime in the Kindergarten Room

Heat, intense as the fragrance of September hibiscus,
fills the kindergarten classroom in the new brick school.
Alphabet carpet tiles cover the floor.
Child-sized mats stacked like lonely rafts in the back of the room. A boy
rolls a blue marble from palm to palm. The curve of a smile paints his face
when our eyes exchange hello. The lights in the room are cut off,
a pedestal fan sweeps the room haltingly. The air still, flat, heavy.
The children take reluctant naps, their damp faces
resting on folded arms atop small, round tables.
What is the logic of kindergarten children napping at tables?
Their teacher, Miss Kimberly, sees the question forming on my face,
pulls up a chair for me at her desk. *This school was built over a landfill.*
There are roaches everywhere. I've even seen them
crawling out of the kids' lunchboxes. I have a mat for each child,
but I'd never let them sleep on this floor. Miss Kimberly checks her watch.
She knows I'm there to pick up several children for the speech class.
Lucky you — with an office out in the trailer.
I don't think we have any roaches out there.

No B.A.R.K.ing in the Hallways

Every day Mrs. Murphy walks down the hallway,
glances at the grinning bulldog mascot
reminding teachers, reminding the students of the school motto

Behavior Attitude Respect Kindness

Mrs. Murphy gives the students paper dog bones
for finishing homework, for being polite, for not teasing Tammy
who lives in a crowded shelter
and smells because she can only shower once a week.

Mrs. Murphy drops duplicate tokens in a box
for the administrators.
They tell her it's for prizes.
She knows better—the duplicates are to judge her compliance.

Behavior Attitude Respect Kindness

She knows there are kids who never earn rewards—
they've given up.
Like Marty. Shouldn't she reward his creativity?
His innovative designs for hydrogen engines?
Marty never finishes his work. He tells her,
I wish I had a class where I could build what I design.

Behavior Attitude Respect Kindness

Marty walks out of class. He knows the odds.
1257 students. Ten prizes a week.
Standing in front of her empty classroom,
Mrs. Murphy sees the futility of the fake rewards.

I hate the whole system and I don't know how many more days
I can tell my students to
BARK in the hallway, BARK in the gym, and BARK in the classroom.

As her students file into the room,
Mrs. Murphy tells them,
Don't forget to save your dog bones for the weekly drawing.

No Dreams for Damien

I sense it the first time I see him—
fear chills me. I shuffle my papers
and stand closer to the board.

He doesn't say much
besides *I hate you* and
Why don't you retire?

Damien challenges everything I say
and something in his slow stare
warns me to watch out.

I dance a familiar routine,
smile, joke, set limits—these usually work
until Damien cusses me out,

refuses to do any work. All my options exhausted,
I call for security.
He rises—all 6'2" lean and coiled,
adjusts an Elmer Fudd bomber hat

low over his eyes, and threatens,
If I see you outside of school,
I'm gonna put my hands on you.

I freeze inside. We stand face-to-face
and I am aware of his posture announcing
that he already knows the world.

His grabs a copy of *A Raisin in the Sun*,
then looks at the board where I have a poster
of the poem "A Dream Deferred."

My dream, Damien whispers, *is to live to be twenty-one.*

Rena's Plan

Rena's brown eyes focus on something in the distance—
she slumps in her chair, cropped brown hair frames her frozen face.
Rena never smiles
except when she talks about going back to Brazil

or about taking care of her five-year-old sister.
They make castles together and later Rena writes stories
with a hero named Marvelous Maggie.
Rena tells me *I love reading to Maggie and writing stories.*
A smile spills across her face.

Rena fails every class in tenth grade—
despite repeating ninth-grade work.
At midterm, she begs for the chance to take Honors English 10.
I'm bored. If you challenge me, I'll work, she promises.
When I ask Rena how she's doing,
she looks past me, then shuts her eyes.
My parents work all the time, so I have to take care of my sister.
I want to take a drawing class. Have you seen my sketch book?

"Rena, your illustrations are gorgeous."
I circle back to the academics.
"How's it going in English?"
I missed a test because I was sick, but I'll make it up this week.
I'm doing great. Rena doesn't reveal her D average.
I'm going to Brazil in January, so none of this matters.

Rena's hair is shorter every time I see her.
She sports a studded leather collar around her neck,
wears baggy tee shirts with old Punk band logos. She holds hands
with a girl when she walks out of school.

I used to want to kill myself, and I've been feeling really sad
again. I don't think I'm going to hurt myself, but I'm afraid.
Rena refuses to speak to me because I tell her parents what she said.
She turns away when I approach. She continues to fail every class.

Rena shaves all of her hair and leaves a long strip,
hanging over one eye.
She dyes it green. I see her hugging a girl in the hallway.
Rena's clothes more masculine, her face impassive, yet defiant.

My parents won't let me go to Brazil, she tells me.
I'm dropping out.

Ricky's Smile

Ricky wears frayed tee shirts with Big Bird and Ernie.
"I love Thethame Thtreet," he giggles.

His feet barely touch the floor when he sits in the speech room,
red Chucks swinging back and forth as he shuffles the cards.

Ricky chooses five pictures from the deck, lines them up,
then tells me a story—pronouncing each "s" word correctly—

his wide grin revealing yellowing
front teeth etched with tooth decay's thick black lines.

Concerned, I schedule a conference.
Ricky's mother takes both of my hands in hers, speaks softly.

I'm so glad to meet you. Ricky loves your class.
Ricky's mother smiles. I gulp, freeze inside.

She has no front teeth.
Why did you want to see me?

Robbie's Mother Gets the Message

It was easier before I had my own children,
before I saw my blond son and brunette daughter
as extensions of myself.
Before I knew about the secret dream box
every parent tucks their wishes into, brimming
with bright futures, blossoming talent.

I remember the first time I sat in a room with Robbie's mother
who wanted to know why her nearly seven-year-old son
couldn't read the color words,
couldn't form his letters legibly,
or zip his own jacket.

In that cramped room with the little chairs
all of us sitting around the table—the psychologist,
the team leader, the principal, and me—the teacher.
Married without children.

Somehow all the test results made sense
of Robbie's slow physical growth and charming silliness
so typical of a much younger child. And how even the
graying psychologist seemed tentative instead of clinical when she spoke:

"Robbie's a sweet boy with lots of potential, but
it's going to take him much longer to learn...he'll probably struggle..."

I can still feel the air, heavy and still, my shock
when Robbie's mother pushed back from the table,
cut through all the jargon and said,
You mean my son is retarded.

Roxie Hates Losers

None of us like you, lady.
Your class is lame. You better not fail me
like all them other losers in my life.
Like my stepmother.
Last night she chased my dad out of the house.
He was drunk again. Damned alcoholic.
He's got that liver thing—cyrannosis—whatever.
Then he wrapped his car around a tree so it hooked like a staple.
Alcoholics—I hate them all.

And now you expect me to study for a vocabulary test?

Roxie leans back and stretches out her legs, then props her feet on the chair,
lifting her hoodie to check on her new belly piercing.
Two boys next to her grin.
Hey, guys, wanna touch my new piercing? Yeah, I don't think so.
Keep your grubby paws off me.

When the bell rings,
Roxie kicks the file cabinet on her way out of the room.

Ryan's Secret

Some days I think about Ryan
a fifteen-year-old I tutored for dyslexia.
I remember how he rested his head on the desk,
how his eyes slowly closed in the middle of lessons,
and how he blamed his fatigue on insomnia.
Ryan's story came back to me
as I listened to a radio show
about a website called *PostSecret*
where secrets are printed on postcards and shared all over the web.

One postcard was from a teen who was terrorized
in the middle of the night because
parents, siblings broke down her bedroom door.
Once her postcard was published,
the website was flooded
with more secrets of broken doors and stolen safety.

And I remember the day Ryan broke down
and confessed that his twin brother Miles
— taller and forty pounds heavier —
broke the lock on his bedroom door,
then tore it off the hinges.
Miles hits my dad, too, even though he's blind.
Ryan asked me for help.
I know Miles abuses us, but he's my brother. I love him.

I told the principal and his assistant.

The principal took off his glasses, looked down at the floor.
"It won't do any good to report that."

Sometimes a Poet

strays from describing the crescent moon
as a wedge of dawn light
and stares into the confused faces
of her students as they struggle against
the sharp edges of learning parts of speech.

Elusive nouns—do they sidle up
to adverbs or pronouns?
My students plunge over and over
into the murky water of language,
then break their pencils in frustration.

Still reaching for success,
my students crack the code
when they read preposition poems—
the concrete awareness of describing
where things are.
One by one
they share their poems.

"Out of the car
bags in my arms
through the doorway
put the groceries
into the cabinets."

But Michael sits silent in the back of the room.
I'll never know if he wanted praise or relief
when he placed his poem in front of me
and waited silently as I read it.

On the deep streets
of West Baltimore
my friend lies bleeding
under a car.

Sparring Partners

Chas in the hoodie
stands coiled and ready,
a boxer anticipating a left hook
right jab.
He murmurs a vibrato stream
of hushed cuss words.
Bastard coaches just don't know talent.
Uppercut, jab.
I'm better than all them shit-faced guys
who made the team.
I'll show them.

His brown eyes peer at me under the hoodie.
What you lookin' at, lady? he sneers.
My easy hello catches him off-guard,
then I slip in a sidewinder punch of news.
"We're going to work on passing that high school exit exam."
I ain't doin' no writin' and readin' crap.
Chas tells me
Besides, I can't pass no tests.

But when I step into the ring
and go a few rounds of one-to-one tutoring with Chas,
he gradually eases out of his hunched pose.
His *I can't* morphs into *I'll show them.*
Chas in the hoodie
takes off his gloves
for a one-two victory jog.
He struts across the stage
and raises his diploma in his fist.

Teaching Sewing in the Psych Hospital

I don't remember which came first,
the idea of teaching teens to sew
or my raging impatience with the boring lessons
presented by the previous teacher.

Something propelled me to investigate
the old sewing machines buried in the dark cabinets
of my classroom. One day after school
I set each one up, then threaded and tested them.
After being oiled in the right places
all but one worked, ready for service.

"Those kids are dangerous," everyone warns me.
"How can you give them scissors and pins?"
I give them knives in the kitchen......cooking's
not too dangerous to teach them. I teach cooking.

Did I ask what should I do with them next?
My eight teens, all bound in the invisible chains
of depression, rage, and fear.
What made me think I could teach them to sew?

They love the idea of the Linus Project—
joining the army of stitchers making blankets for homeless people
or premature babies.
"My girlfriend is pregnant," Danny announces,
"I say we make baby blankets."
"I can sew," Billy tells me, "I'll help you teach."

The soft fabrics soothe the aches and fears
my students carry like heavy backpacks.
These weary teens with jailed fathers
and drug-addicted siblings
find solace in the hum of the sewing machines,
the noiseless up and down of hand-stitching.

These kids who rage against any structure the school imposes
now happy, content,
tie embroidery floss to quilt the layers,
making blankets
for all those unseen babies.

Teacher's Survival Kit

It's never as simple as bringing in fresh flowers for your desk or hanging an inspirational poster. Instead you turn to the invisible, the metaphysical. Your nightly meditations suffused with mantras about letting go. Breathe in positive, breathe out fear when you work with Marvene of the Ambush. You follow simple rules. Keep a half-smile on your face because it feels hopeful. Spray the classroom with Five Flower Essence. Fill the room with white light before class with the girl who brags about making you cry. Pull an angel card with a praise word for the boy who asks, *When are you going to retire?* Take the class full of high school boys on a walk when they can't focus for more than five minutes. Follow the trail around the school, over the creek. You tell them that walking discharges energy, which is true enough. But you know that walking is the way you hold onto hope on those days when the pace of teaching class after class of emotionally disturbed teens with learning disabilities hits you like a meteor and your patience pales with each fresh peril the bell brings.

You want to dwell in possibility
so you imagine a field full of sunflowers.

The Autoworker and the Factory Model

We never stopped the line,
no matter what mistakes we saw.
We worked a lot of overtime fixing mistakes
but we never stopped the line. "This American Life," 2010

And I feel the same way about Ben,
my student determined to graduate from high school
still reading at the third- or fourth-grade level.

The administrators say,
Ben needs credits to graduate,
and reading class doesn't count
if he takes it more than once.

So administrators find ways
for teachers to push him along,
like the auto factory grinding out
a Ford Focus with Fiesta doors
held on by Explorer bolts.

Nothing fits, and you can't drive the car,
but we don't stop the line
for Ben who understands a lot about history
but doesn't read well enough to take the test.

So we give him an accommodation—special help—
and someone reads him the test,
which worked well when he was seven
but seems foolish when he is seventeen—
and hoping to get a job, hoping to graduate.
So I ask, *Will someone read to Ben at work?*

The answer echoes back *We can't stop the line.*
But when you peek under the hood —
like the car with the wrong bolts,
Ben will need repairs.

The Northern Way

My supervisor, Mrs. Wyeth, waits inside the trailer for me.
I'm here today to see how you're getting along.
This being your first year and all. Just a little informal observation.
Her Southern speech—bourbon-smooth with a hint of ice.

"This is Benjie," I introduce the little boy by my side.
"We're working on the 's' sound."
Hey, Benjie, Mrs. Wyeth coos, *give me a big smile.*
Benjie grins—a jack-o'lantern space where his
front teeth were only last week. The last time I saw him.

My stomach plunges. Even I know I've messed up.
Jotting a few notes on her paper, Mrs. Wyeth pats my hand
and shakes her head. *I don't know about those Northern ways*
of yours, but here in Richmond, we wait till a child's teeth come in
before working on that 's' sound.

The Testing Game

Kathy, my special education supervisor, explained her logic.
 "We can't classify Horace as cognitively impaired.
His new scores in two subtests are too high—
cognitive impairment is 70 and below.
Horace's new score is 71."

But all of his other scores are only in the 60s—a sign of cognitive impairment.
He scored at the first-grade level in reading,
and the third-grade level in math.
How is that average for a fifteen-year-old?

Kathy sighed, then adjusted the beads on her bracelet.
"Horace is a "tweener"— too high for a life skills class,
too low for college prep,
but at least he'll be socialized with his peers."

She continued.
"He'll take the high school assessments needed for graduation,
fail them a few times,
then we can give him a certificate of attendance.
That way, we can skip the red tape."

I felt sick and angry,
but spoke calmly.
What about Horace?
Think about what all of that failure will do to his spirit.

Kathy closed her book, looked at her watch—ready to move on.
"We have more and more 'tweeners' every year,
but no programs for them."
Before I could ask the obvious question—
Why don't we have any programs?—

Kathy recited her speech.
"The most important thing is that he'll be with his peers.
Then we can skip the hassle of giving alternative assessments.
They mess up our data."

After a final glance at her watch,
Kathy shoved all of her files into a new Coach bag
and shrugged her shoulders.
"It's up to you to tell his mother."

All I had was a twist on some special ed-speak to throw back at her.
We might be offering Horace a free education,
but it's not an appropriate education.

Kathy managed a weak smile, shrugged her shoulders, and took off.
My mind raced. *What about Horace?*
How will I handle the conversation with his mother?

I told her the truth—how the new score was determined
and explained what a certificate of attendance could mean for Horace.
He'll be able to get a job, but probably won't be able to pass a GED.
His reading level is too low. And Horace resists every effort I make to help him.

Horace's mother slumped
under the weight of all this—
I wanted to hug her.

And even as I told her about Horace's new situation,
I knew that the inadequate education offered to Horace
was also the reality for thousands of other Maryland students.

Horace dropped out of high school in his sophomore year
along with several other "tweeners."
Does Kathy ever think about that?

(The Individuals with Disabilities Education Act [IDEA] dictates that
every student identified as a special education student is entitled to a
"free and appropriate public education [FAPE]")

(High School Assessments: Maryland's high school graduation tests needed to earn a diploma, in use before the PARCC tests)

(Life skills class teaches basic things like following directions and reading signs, while regular education classes have a college-prep curriculum.)

The Voices in My Ear

Based on: "Why are urban teachers being trained to be robots?"
by Amy Berand, which details her experiences with training by
the Center for Transformational Teaching's approach to discipline
called No Nonsense Nurturing (NNN).

There are four adults in my classroom—
three coach me on "No Nonsense Nurturing"
from the back of the room where they share a walkie-talkie.
I wear an earpiece so I can hear what they tell me to do.
I don't have a mouthpiece.

When my students enter the room, my instructors tell me to say,
"In seats, zero talking, page six, questions one to four."
I don't even talk to my dog like that.
They tell me that reporting every detail of student behavior
holds the key to the "No Nonsense Nurturing" teaching style.
Noel is finishing question three. Marjorie is sitting silently.

In the front of the room
an excited sixth-grader
speaks out of turn again.
"Give him a warning,"
says the voice in my earpiece from the back of the room.
I obey. I speak in the monotone I am coached to use.
 "Tell him he has a detention," the voice directs.

The boy stands up,
points to the three coaches
huddled around the walkie-talkie
in the back of the room.
He implores me—

"Miss, don't listen to them! You be you!
Talk to me! I'm a person.
Be a person, Miss.
Be you."

I struggle to adopt the emotionless tone
that No Nonsense Nurturing requires.
The people with walkie-talkies say,
"You appear too happy."
They tell me to stand in mountain pose,
to stop conveying so much excitement.

Oh, I'm sorry, I blurt.
The student tells me,
"Don't apologize for being nice.
"Don't do what those voices say."
"I like you just how you are, Miss."

"Be a person, Miss."
"Be you."

William Who Reverses

William who reverses
b and d
p and q
hides behind bored stares and backwards hats, then
smiles as he describes rebuilding engines,
trouble-shooting heating and air systems.
William reverses
cad and *cab*
then lays his head on the desk and sighs. *I don't know.*
Honest, I just don't know.
When I ask him about school, he looks down
at his shoes, mumbles *It's fine.*
I shuffle some papers. The silence prompts him to speak.
Really, nothing I read makes sense. I do a lot of guessing.
All year long William shows up for reading class every day.
He reads syllable by syllable
re ject ion
pro ject ion
inter ject ion
William smiles when he can *finally* spell,
the patterns on the page suddenly as clear as the parts of an engine.
One day William grins at me and pulls out his cell phone.
Did I tell you? I'm playing Words with Friends now.

Zeke's Mask

Zeke wears his uniform
black leather jacket, black hair,
chains hanging from hip pockets,
black boots.
Won't talk in class,
says he can't write
unless I sit next to him
and prompt word by painful word.
He draws guns all over his books.
The social worker warns me—
"He's crazy.
He set fire to a trailer one day.
He's dangerous—
watch out."

What no one tells me
is that Zeke was six years old,
alone every day in the trailer.
His mother left him every morning at five.
She worked as a waitress
and called him on the phone
to wake him for school.
Zeke set fire to the trailer.
Six-year-old boy
alone, all day.
Still sitting behind that
head-down, "dare-me-to-try" mask.
He's crazy.

Wingless Bird

I'm trying to imagine a wingless bird
stranded in the tangle of a garden.
Could he sing me awake in the morning?
His hollow-boned body unbalanced, frail.

And then I am in the classroom with my students,
no longer allowed the freedom to wander
the gardens of their dreams,
arrested souls forced onto the conveyer belt

of the public schools.
Relentlessly moving
toward the same invisible goal.
If my school were like a garden

there would be shaded places to pause,
to touch pink flower petals,
lift the blossoms to your face,
follow the flight of a honeybee.

But on the production line
that is the modern school
one question remains—

Who will thrive
and who will fly?

About the Author

Ann Bracken is a writer, educator, and expressive arts consultant whose poetry, essays, and interviews have appeared in *Little Patuxent Review*, *Life in Me Like Grass on Fire: Love Poems*, *Reckless Writing Anthology: Emerging Poets of the 21st Century*, *Women Write Resistance: Poets Resist Gender Violence*, *Pif Magazine*, *New Verse News*, and *Arlijo* among others. Ann Bracken's poems were twice nominated for the Pushcart Prize. She serves as the deputy editor for *Little Patuxent Review* and leads workshops at creativity conferences, including Florida Creativity and The Creative Problem Solving Institute. She is the founder of the Possibility Project, which offers expressive arts and creativity workshops for people of all ages, as well as poetry and writing workshops in prisons and schools. Ann has two grown children and lives in Columbia, MD.

Author photo on back cover by Cheryl Fair, 2013.

CPSIA information can be obtained
at www.ICGtesting.com
Printed in the USA
BVOW08s2319110617
486548BV00001B/9/P